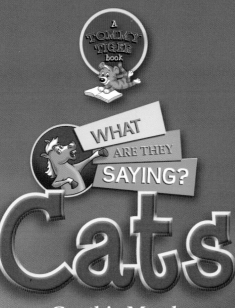

A TOMMY TIGER book

WHAT ARE THEY SAYING?

Cats

Cynthia Mead

PURPLE TOAD PUBLISHING

P.O. Box 631
Kennett Square, PA 19348
www.purpletoadpublishing.com

Printing   1   2   3   4   5   6   7   8   9

WHAT ARE THEY SAYING?
Cats
Dogs
Horses
Guinea Pigs
Birds

Publisher's Cataloging-in-Publication Data
Mead, Cynthia
    What Are They Saying: Cats / Cynthia Mead
        p. cm. — (What are they saying?)
Includes bibliographic references and index.
ISBN: 978-1-62469-083-9 (library bound)
1. Cats—Juvenile literature.   I. Title.
 SF445.7 2013
 636.8 — dc23

2013946337

eBook ISBN: 9781624690846

ABOUT THE AUTHOR: Cynthia Mead has been a cat lover all her life. Born in Chicago, Illinois, she has studied her furry friends through her years living in Italy, California, and the farmlands of Pennsylvania where she now lives with her husband, son, and three feline contributors to this book.

Printed by Lake Book Manufacturing, Chicago, Il.

Cats

When sunlight peeks through the curtain,
I wake up because I am hungry.
I need to wake up my friend.

I tap her with my velvet paw. "Wake up," I say,
but it sounds like, "MEWWWW!"
She rolls over still asleep.
I don't give up!

Pet Fact:

Cats sleep at least 16 hours a day, but they can adapt to your schedule!

"MEEP," I say again like a hungry kitten would to its mommy.
When the message doesn't get through, I help myself. That works!

My eyes blink in love for my friend. We always have breakfast together, but her food never smells as nice as mine.

Pet Fact:

Long, low "meows" can mean your cat is angry whereas shorter and higher ones are friendly.

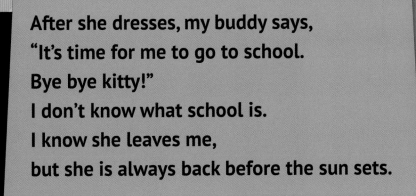

After she dresses, my buddy says,
"It's time for me to go to school.
Bye bye kitty!"
I don't know what school is.
I know she leaves me,
but she is always back before the sun sets.

Pet Fact:

"Meow" is like the Hawaiian word "aloha." It can mean hello as well as goodbye.

Now its time to play with my favorite toy.
It really is amazing how it always waits for me to
try to catch it, but I let it win sometimes, too. I can
do this for hours!

Pet Fact:

Cats often meow to start play, petting, or to get you to talk to them.

Some early morning visitors drop by in the backyard. We try to touch noses, but that glass door is in the way!

Pet Fact:

Cats love to greet friends by touching their noses to them.

I try to chat with them, but they don't speak kitty. I just smile and point the way out of our yard. They seem thankful.

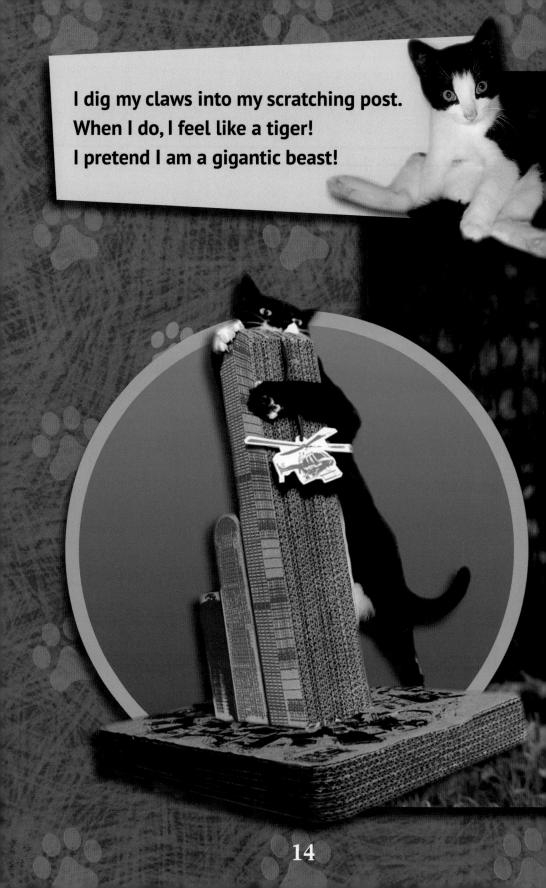

I dig my claws into my scratching post.
When I do, I feel like a tiger!
I pretend I am a gigantic beast!

Pet Fact:

Cats like to scratch to leave scents that other cats can smell.

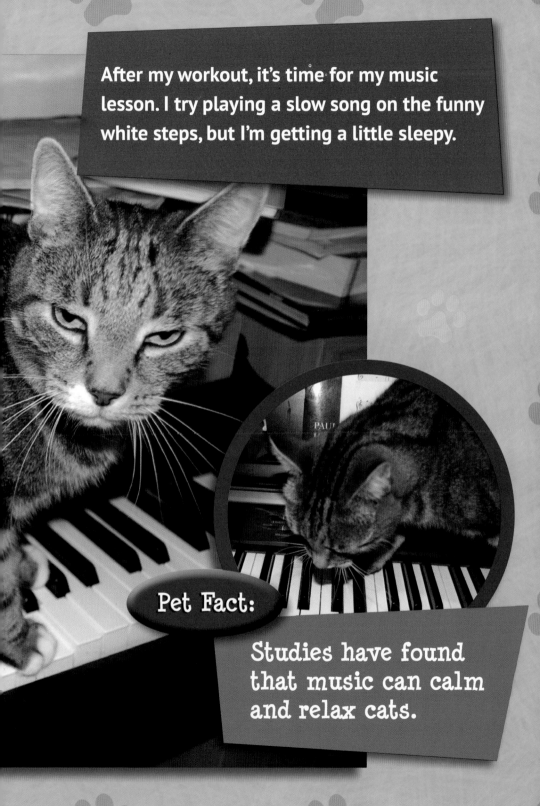

After my workout, it's time for my music lesson. I try playing a slow song on the funny white steps, but I'm getting a little sleepy.

Pet Fact:

Studies have found that music can calm and relax cats.

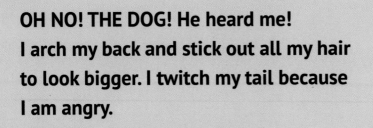

OH NO! THE DOG! He heard me!
I arch my back and stick out all my hair
to look bigger. I twitch my tail because
I am angry.

YOWWWL! I howl my feelings!
HISSSSSSSSSSSSSSSSSSSSSSSSS!
That will show him who is boss!

Pet Fact:

A cat's hiss is a
warning to back away.

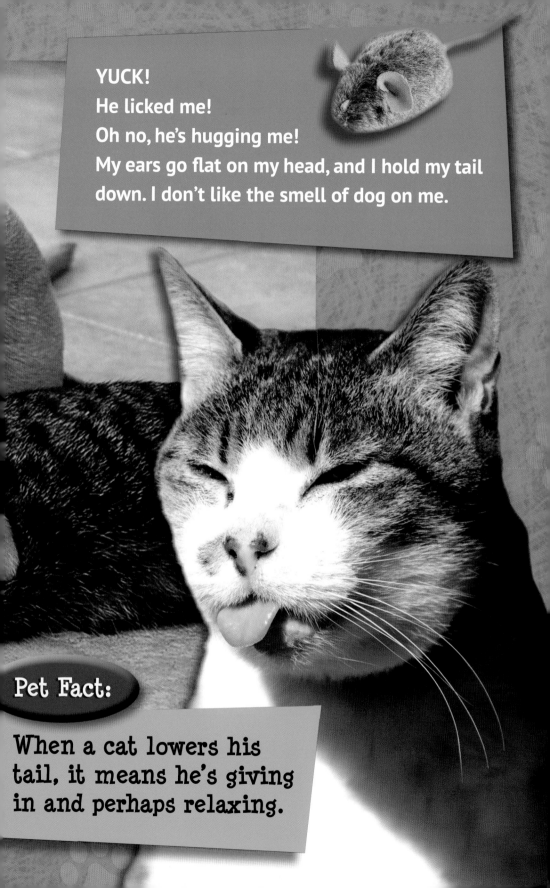

YUCK!
He licked me!
Oh no, he's hugging me!
My ears go flat on my head, and I hold my tail down. I don't like the smell of dog on me.

Pet Fact:

When a cat lowers his tail, it means he's giving in and perhaps relaxing.

I'd better wash myself after that! There's nothing like a tongue bath to stay clean.

Pet Fact:

Cat's tongues are covered with papillae (tiny spines) that work like combs when a cat licks its fur. They feel rough if your kitty licks you!

Time for my buddy to come home!
Somehow I just know. I can hear the school bus way
before it pulls up to our front door. I prick up my ears,
and my tail stands straight up with happiness.

I rub my cheeks on her ankles when she
comes in the house because I love her so much.

Pet Fact:

Cats mark you as their own
by rubbing their cheeks
against you with their
scent glands.

She takes a whiff of me and the next thing I know, she plops me into the sink! Doesn't she know I just gave myself a bath? I guess I still smell like dog breath!

Pet Fact:

Like some kids, some cats hate baths, too. Let an adult help you bathe your cat so you don't get a scratch.

Soon it's my buddy's turn, but she doesn't mind. She actually likes it taking baths! I watch her carefully, though. Those little foamy things could swallow her up!

Later, she combs me gently from head to tail. This is nice. The next time I give myself a bath I will get fewer hairs in my mouth.

Now it's bedtime.
She pets me and I purr.
I knead.
Right paw, left paw.
Right paw, left paw.
Velvet paws, no claws!
I keep them tucked in.
I kiss her hand.
She says, "I love you."
I say, "I love you, too."
But it sounds like
"PURRRRRRRRRRRRR".

Books

Crisp, Marty. *Everything Cat: What Kids Really Want to Know about Cats.* Minnetonka, MN: NorthWord Books for Young Readers, 2003.

Farjeon, Eleanor. *Cats Sleep Anywhere.* Islington, London: Frances Lincoln Children's Books, 2010.

Nagelschneider, Mieshelle. *The Cat Whisperer: Why Cats Do What They Do – and How to Get Them to Do What You Want.* New York: Bantam Books, 2013.

Tabor, Roger. *Understanding Cat Behavior.* Devon, UK: David & Charles, 2003.

Works Consulted

Gutman, Bill. *Becoming Your Cat's Best Friend.* Brookfield, CT: The Millbrook Press, 1997.

Hotchner, Tracie. *The Cat Bible: Everything Your Cat Expects You to Know.* New York: Gotham, 2007.

Johnson-Bennett, Pam. *Think Like a Cat: How to Raise a Well-Adjusted Cat – Not a Sour Puss.* New York: Penguin Books, 2011.

On the Internet

CFA for Kids: About Cats
http://kids.cfa.org

Kittenwar
http://kittenwar.com

National Geographic Kids
http://kids.nationalgeographic.com/

INDEX

aloha 8

angry 6

ankles 25

arch 19

blinking 6

claws 30

combing 29

ears 20

glands 25

hiss 18

meow 6, 9

music 16

nose 12

papillae 22

play 10

purr 30

scents 15, 25

schedule 4

scratch 15

scratching 14

sunlight 4

tail 20

tiger 14

tongue 22